JOHN 13–21

Part 2: The Way to True Life

13 STUDIES FOR INDIVIDUALS OR GROUPS

LifeGuide®
BIBLE STUDIES

DOUGLAS CONNELLY

ivp

An imprint of InterVarsity Press
Downers Grove, Illinois

To Jon

InterVarsity Press
P.O. Box 1400, Downers Grove, IL 60515-1426
ivpress.com
email@ivpress.com

©1990, 2002 by Douglas Connelly

InterVarsity Press® is the book-publishing division of InterVarsity Christian Fellowship/USA®, a movement of students and faculty active on campus at hundreds of universities, colleges and schools of nursing in the United States of America, and a member movement of the International Fellowship of Evangelical Students. For information about local and regional activities, visit intervarsity.org.

LifeGuide® is a registered trademark of InterVarsity Christian Fellowship.

All Scripture quotations, unless otherwise indicated, are taken from the Holy Bible, New International Version®. NIV®. Copyright ©1973, 1978, 1984 by International Bible Society. Used by permission of Zondervan Publishing House. All rights reserved.

Cover design: Cindy Kiple
Interior design: Jeanna Wiggins
Cover image: Lake: © Paulo Dias / Trevillion Images

ISBN 978-0-8308-3122-7 (print)
ISBN 978-0-8308-6207-8 (digital)

Printed in the United States of America ∞

InterVarsity Press is committed to ecological stewardship and to the conservation of natural resources in all our operations. This book was printed using sustainably sourced paper.

P	15	14	13	12	11	10	9	8	7	6	5	4	3	2
Y	34	33	32	31	30	29	28	27	26	25	24	23	22	

CONTENTS

GETTING THE MOST OUT OF JOHN 13–21

T he most significant fact in history can be summed up in four words: *Jesus Christ is God!*

The great declaration of the Bible is that God in human flesh was born in Bethlehem. It was God in the person of Jesus Christ who astonished the people of his day with his miracles and amazed them with his teaching. It was God who lived a perfect life and then allowed himself to be put to death on a Roman cross for humanity's sins. It was God who broke the bonds of death three days after he died and came out of the grave alive. The deity of Jesus—the fact that he was God in human form—is the bottom line of the Christian faith.

When the apostle John sat down to write his Gospel, he was not interested simply in adding one more account of Jesus' life to the three already in existence. John wrote his book with a very specific purpose in mind:

> Jesus did many other miraculous signs in the presence of his disciples, which are not recorded in this book. But these are written that you may believe that Jesus is the Christ, the Son of God, and that by believing you may have life in his name. (John 20:30-31)

John's book is not a biography; it's a theological argument. John wants to convince us that Jesus of Nazareth is God the Son. Then he wants to show us how that fact will change our lives in some amazing ways. It is by believing in Jesus Christ as the Son of God that we find life—real life, eternal life, a whole new kind of life!

Every event John records is designed to show us that Jesus is God. John pulls from the life of Jesus specific incidents that demonstrate his majesty and deity. Of particular interest to John are the sign miracles of

Jesus. In the first twelve chapters of his book he records seven miracles. These miracles were not performed simply to relieve human suffering or to meet human needs; they were "signs." They pointed to the truth of Jesus' claim to be the Son of God.

John was the last Gospel writer. The best evidence points to a date around A.D. 90 for the composition of his Gospel. The other Gospels had been in circulation for some time. John wrote to add his unique perspective and to fill in some of the details not recorded by the other writers. He assumes his readers are familiar with the other Gospels. John does not mention, for example, the anguish of Jesus in the Garden of Gethsemane. The other writers had adequately described that incident. John does, however, give us the details of Jesus' conversation with his disciples on the night before his crucifixion. The other writers mention it only briefly.

John never mentions himself by name in the Gospel; he refers to himself simply as "the disciple whom Jesus loved." We have in this Gospel the memories of an intimate friend about Jesus. Jesus had transformed John's life. I hope you are prepared to have that happen to you! You are about to begin a fascinating study focused on the greatest person who ever lived—Jesus Christ. If you will respond to what John writes in faith and obedience, you, like John, will experience a whole new kind of life.

SUGGESTIONS FOR INDIVIDUAL STUDY

1. As you begin each study, pray that God will speak to you through his Word.

2. Read the introduction to the study and respond to the personal reflection question or exercise. This is designed to help you focus on God and on the theme of the study.

3. Each study deals with a particular passage—so that you can delve into the author's meaning in that context. Read and reread the passage to be studied. The questions are written using the language of the New International Version, so you may wish to use that version of the Bible. The New Revised Standard Version is also recommended.

4. This is an inductive Bible study, designed to help you discover for yourself what Scripture is saying. The study includes three types of questions. *Observation* questions ask about the basic facts: who, what, when, where and how. *Interpretation* questions delve into the meaning of the passage. *Application* questions help you discover the implications of the text for growing in Christ. These three keys unlock the treasures of Scripture.

Write your answers to the questions in the spaces provided or in a personal journal. Writing can bring clarity and deeper understanding of yourself and of God's Word.

5. It might be good to have a Bible dictionary handy. Use it to look up any unfamiliar words, names or places.

6. Use the prayer suggestion to guide you in thanking God for what you have learned and to pray about the applications that have come to mind.

7. You may want to go on to the suggestion under "Now or Later," or you may want to use that idea for your next study.

SUGGESTIONS FOR MEMBERS OF A GROUP STUDY

1. Come to the study prepared. Follow the suggestions for individual study mentioned above. You will find that careful preparation will greatly enrich your time spent in group discussion.

2. Be willing to participate in the discussion. The leader of your group will not be lecturing. Instead, he or she will be encouraging the members of the group to discuss what they have learned. The leader will be asking the questions that are found in this guide.

3. Stick to the topic being discussed. Your answers should be based on the verses which are the focus of the discussion and not on outside authorities such as commentaries or speakers. These studies focus on a particular passage of Scripture. Only rarely should you refer to other portions of the Bible. This allows for everyone to participate in in-depth study on equal ground.

4. Be sensitive to the other members of the group. Listen attentively when they describe what they have learned. You may be surprised by their insights! Each question assumes a variety of answers. Many questions do not have "right" answers, particularly questions that aim at meaning or application. Instead the questions push us to explore the passage more thoroughly.

When possible, link what you say to the comments of others. Also, be affirming whenever you can. This will encourage some of the more hesitant members of the group to participate.

5. Be careful not to dominate the discussion. We are sometimes so eager to express our thoughts that we leave too little opportunity for others to respond. By all means participate! But allow others to also.

6. Expect God to teach you through the passage being discussed and through the other members of the group. Pray that you will have an enjoyable and profitable time together, but also that as a result of the study you will find ways that you can take action individually and/or as a group.

7. Remember that anything said in the group is considered confidential and should not be discussed outside the group unless specific permission is given to do so.

8. If you are the group leader, you will find additional suggestions at the back of the guide.

ONE

THE SON AS A SLAVE

John 13:1-17

There were two things on Jesus' heart the night before his crucifixion—his Father and his disciples. In chapters 13—17 of John we have the privilege of listening to his conversations with them both. Before Jesus can instruct his disciples about his death, however, he has to act out a lesson in servitude.

Group Discussion. Have you ever been asked to do a demeaning, lowly job? What thoughts went through your mind at that time?

Personal Reflection. Do you feel awkward or uncomfortable when others try to serve you? Why or why not?

In this passage Jesus shows us the spirit he expects in those who follow him. Greatness in Jesus' eyes does not come from having many servants but from being the servant of many. *Read John 13:1-17.*

1. According to John, what does Jesus know about himself (vv. 1-3)?

2. In light of that knowledge, what is remarkable about what Jesus does next (vv. 4-5)?

3. Footwashing was normally done by servants or slaves. Why do you think Jesus washes his disciples' feet instead of simply giving them a sermon on love?

4. What tasks at home, at work or in church would be equivalent to footwashing?

5. How do you think Jesus feels as he washes Judas's feet?

How do you think Judas feels?

6. Is Peter simply being humble when he refuses to allow Jesus to serve him (vv. 6-8)? Explain your answer.

7. What spiritual truth is Jesus trying to communicate to Peter (and to us) in verses 8-11?

8. After he finishes washing the disciples' feet, how does Jesus explain the significance of his actions (vv. 12-17)?

9. What does this chapter reveal to you about your attitude toward serving?

10. Among the people you live and work with, what would it mean to "practice footwashing"—to model the humility of Jesus?

 Ask God to cultivate a humble spirit in you.

NOW OR LATER

When we think of great people we don't usually include servants on our list. But in Jesus' kingdom the ways of the world are often reversed. The place of honor in Jesus' organizational "pyramid" is not toward the top. Instead the pyramid is turned over on its point. What counts is not how many people are "under" your authority but how many people you serve in love (see Matthew 20:26-27). Envision how your workplace or home would operate differently if that servant mentality was a consistent reality.

TWO

A TRAITOR?
NOT ME!

John 13:18-38

W e all knew Bill was a snitch. Any comment he could twist into a criticism or complaint, any action he could portray as a breach of company policy was reported to our boss within minutes. Bill couldn't be trusted!

Group Discussion. If you knew a close friend was going to falsely betray you, and the betrayal would cost you your job, what would you do?

Personal Reflection. Has someone in your life ever hurt you deeply? What was your response to him or her?

If we had been one of Jesus' disciples, we would probably have found it difficult to be around Peter. He was blunt and, at times, arrogant. On the other hand, we might have regarded Judas with trust and respect. The only one who saw deeply enough to discern the true character of these men was Jesus. *Read John 13:18-38.*

| **1.** What tone of voice do you think Jesus uses in verse 21?

| in verse 26?

in verse 27?

2. Evidently the disciples did not know who would betray Jesus (v. 22). What does this tell you about how Jesus had treated Judas?

3. How do the disciples interpret Jesus' instruction to Judas in verse 27 (vv. 28-29)?

4. Can we apply Jesus' example to the way we should treat our "betrayers," or was this a unique situation that really doesn't apply today? Explain your answer.

5. What is "new" about Jesus' command in verse 34?

6. John later wrote, "This is how we know what love is: Jesus Christ laid down his life for us. And we ought to lay down our lives for our brothers" (1 John 3:16). In what practical ways can we exhibit this sacrificial love?

7. Why does that kind of love convince all of humanity that we are Jesus' disciples (v. 35)?

8. Do you think Peter's declaration in verse 37 comes from pride or from sincerity? Explain why you came to that conclusion.

9. Three people stand out in this passage—Jesus, Judas and Peter. What one character quality of each—good or evil—makes the greatest impression of you?

10. What can you do to avoid the failures and to follow after the strengths of each main character?

 Let God speak to you about any areas of spiritual weakness or vulnerability in your life. Pray for a strong faith that will keep you from turning away from the Lord in a crisis.

NOW OR LATER

On a scale of 1 (low) to 10 (exceptional), how does your church or Christian community rank against the standard of love Jesus spells out in verses 34 and 35? What can you do personally to increase the score?

THREE

COMFORT FOR A TROUBLED HEART

John 14

T he call came late at night. A broken sob was followed by these words: "Our son is dying. Will you please come to the hospital?" As I made the trip through darkened streets, I wondered what I could say to bring comfort to these heartbroken parents.

Group Discussion. Who is the person you most want to be around when you are hurting? What is it about that person that brings comfort to you?

Personal Reflection. Think of a friend who is going through a personal crisis. If you were with that person now, how would you try to help him or her?

Jesus faced the challenge of dealing with broken hearts too. In this chapter he comforts eleven disciples who feel like their world is coming unglued. *Read John 14:1-14.*

1. What does Jesus say in chapter 13 that causes his disciples to have "troubled" hearts (v. 1)?

2. How would the promises Jesus makes in verses 1-4 bring comfort to his disciples?

3. After being with Jesus for over three years, what had both Thomas and Philip failed to realize about him (vv. 5-14)?

4. Put Jesus' statement in verses 6 and 7 in your own words. In light of those verses, how would you answer someone who thinks there are "many ways to God"?

5. *Read John 14:15-31.* Another source of comfort for these troubled disciples would be the Holy Spirit. What does the title Counselor (v. 16) tell us about the Spirit's ministry?

6. In what specific ways is the Spirit willing to bring comfort and help in your life (vv. 15-27)?

7. What is the relationship between our love and obedience to Jesus and his love and presence in our lives (vv. 15-24)?

How is this different from legalism—trying to earn Jesus' love and presence through our good works?

8. How does the peace Jesus offers differ from the peace offered by the world (vv. 25-31)?

9. How can Jesus' teaching help you counsel a friend who is going through a crisis or who has a troubled heart?

10. Where do you need Jesus' peace in your life right now?

11. What words of Jesus in this passage are most significant to you personally?

 Give whatever is troubling you to the Lord and wait in his presence for his comfort and peace.

NOW OR LATER

Think of a friend who is going through a difficult time. Plan to do something this week to encourage that person. A phone call, a letter, a small gift, or an invitation to lunch or a sporting event might be a wonderful blessing in his or her life.

FOUR

THE SECRET OF THE VINE

John 15:1-11

The final weekend before Christmas is not the time to visit a shopping mall. If you are fortunate enough to find a parking spot, the press of people inside makes shopping almost impossible. On one expedition I heard a mother giving final instructions to her young son before plunging into the crowd: "Stay close to me and hold my hand all the time. We won't get separated if we hold on to each other."

Group Discussion. When you were a child, did you try to stay close to your parents in an unfamiliar place, or did you tend to wander away? Describe a memory (or fear) of being lost.

Personal Reflection. Have you ever felt far from Christ since becoming a Christian? What circumstances made you feel that way?

As Jesus prepared his disciples to face life without his visible presence, he impressed on them the importance of staying close to him spiritually. He said, "Remain in me." If you've ever longed to understand the secret of spiritual growth, you will find it in Jesus' words to us in John 15. *Read John 15:1-11.*

1. Jesus' instruction to his disciples in this passage revolves around three symbols—the vine, the gardener and the branches. What is Jesus trying to communicate by calling himself the "true vine"?

2. What is the significance of calling his disciples "branches"?

3. Instead of commanding us to bear fruit, why is Jesus' only command "Remain in me" (v. 4)?

4. What does it mean to remain in Christ?

5. The fruit produced by the remaining branch is sometimes viewed as a reference to new converts. But branches produce grapes, not other branches. What other possible meanings are there for *fruit*?

6. The Father's ministry as the gardener is to "[cut] off every branch . . . that bears no fruit" (v. 2). What do you think that means?

7. The Father prunes fruitful branches to make them *more* fruitful (v. 2). In what ways have you experienced the Father's "pruning," and what were the results?

8. What spiritual benefits result from remaining in Christ (vv. 7-11)?

9. There are three categories of branches described in this passage—those bearing no fruit, those bearing some fruit and those bearing much fruit. In which category would you place yourself, and why?

10. If you are not bearing much fruit, what is Jesus' counsel to you in these verses?

 Picture yourself as a vine bearing abundant, healthy fruit. Ask God to help you become the person he desires you to be.

NOW OR LATER

What hesitancy do you have about cultivating your relationship with Jesus?

What are some specific things you can do to deepen your relationship with Jesus?

FIVE

THE COST
OF FRIENDSHIP

John 15:12–16:4

D uring his life on earth, Jesus did not surround himself with a group of students or even a group of followers. He placed himself in the company of friends. I used to think it was a sign of spiritual strength when someone said, "I don't really need other people. I just need the Lord." Now I see it as a sign of immaturity. Close relationships are Christlike!

Group Discussion. What are some of the most important qualities in a friend?

Personal Reflection. Who is your closest friend? Take some time to pray for that person as you begin this study.

As Jesus continues his conversation with his disciples, Jesus shows us what friendship with him is really like. There is both comfort and cost. *Read John 15:12-17.*

1. Jesus already told his disciples to love each other (John 13:34-35). How does his instruction in verse 12 raise the standard of our love?

2. What are the requirements and benefits of friendship with Jesus (vv. 14-17)?

THE COST OF FRIENDSHIP

3. Is being a friend of Jesus the same as being a believer in Jesus? Explain.

4. *Read John 15:18-25.* Why does Jesus switch from talking about love to talk about hate?

5. What reasons does Jesus give for the world's hatred?

6. Give one or two specific examples of how you have experienced the world's hatred as a Christian. How did you respond to the hostility at the time?

7. What does Jesus mean when he says that without his coming, his words and his miracles, the world "would not be guilty of sin" (vv. 22-25)?

8. *Read John 15:26–16:4.* In what ways will the Counselor and the disciples themselves continue the ministry begun by Jesus (vv. 26-27)?

9. What kind of treatment can the disciples expect from those who do not know Christ (16:1-4)?

10. What kinds of persecution are most probable for us in our society? Explain your answer.

11. If we as Christians are not persecuted in some way, what might that imply about our spiritual commitment?

 Pray for strength to face opposition with the same courage and grace that Jesus demonstrated.

NOW OR LATER

Most Christians in democratic societies face very little serious persecution for their faith. Christians in other parts of the world, however, often have to endure imprisonment, poverty, slavery and even death for their commitment to Christ. Check out some websites of organizations that help persecuted Christians. Read some of their literature.
Pray for your brothers and sisters in distress.

SIX

SECRETS
OF THE SPIRIT
John 16:5-15

A lovely woman in our church died not long ago. She knew for almost a year that unless the Lord intervened, the cancer in her brain would kill her. That year gave her time and opportunity to express her love for her husband and family and to say goodbye. She used the hours left of her life to pass on godly wisdom and encouragement to every life she touched.

Group Discussion. How are you at saying goodbye? Is it easier for you to be the person leaving or the person left behind? Why?

Personal Reflection. What would you want to tell your family or closest friends if you knew that you had only a short time to live?

In John 16 Jesus knows that he will die in less than twenty-four hours. When his disciples are faced with that reality, they become troubled (14:1), then afraid (14:27) and finally filled with grief (16:6). Jesus responds to each of their concerns by talking about the coming Holy Spirit. *Read John 16:5-15.*

1. Based on what Jesus says in these verses, how would you describe the mood among the disciples?

How would you have felt if you had been there?

2. Jesus says that it is for the disciples' good that he should leave and that the Counselor should come. Why is the Spirit's presence more profitable to the disciples than Jesus' presence?

3. In what ways is it more profitable today to have the Holy Spirit actively present than to have Jesus here on earth?

4. What does Jesus say the Spirit's ministry would be toward the world (vv. 8-11)?

5. How does the Spirit do the same work today in the hearts of people who have not believed in Jesus?

6. "The prince of this world" mentioned in verse 11 is Satan, our spiritual enemy. In what way does Satan "now stand condemned"?

7. Why is it important for the Holy Spirit to convince the world that its "prince" is already condemned?

8. What can we infer from verses 8-11 about our part in bringing people to faith in Christ?

What is the Spirit's responsibility in bringing people to faith in Christ?

9. One of the Spirit's ministries is communication. What specific things did Jesus say the Spirit would communicate to the disciples (vv. 12-15)?

10. How does the Spirit guide us into God's truth and bring glory to Jesus today?

11. What spiritual truth would you like to ask the Holy Spirit to help you understand?

 Ask God the Holy Spirit to teach you and to exalt Jesus in your life.

NOW OR LATER

One of the roles of the Holy Spirit is to bring glory (as in attention, honor) to Jesus (John 16:14). Do you think your church or Christian fellowship puts too much emphasis on the Holy Spirit, too little emphasis or just about the right emphasis? How can you "test" the Spirit's presence in a worship or praise service?

SEVEN

PEACE IN A TIME OF TROUBLE

John 16:16-33

T hose who follow Jesus are not shielded from life's deepest problems. We must still face sorrow, rejection and heartache. We see our loved ones die, we see relationships fail, and sometimes our children go their own way rather than God's way. What makes a Christian different is not the absence of difficulty but the presence of a Comforter. We never walk life's valleys alone.

Group Discussion. Trace the story of a painful experience in your life. How did God help you during that time of struggle?

Personal Reflection. Who do you turn to first when you are in sorrow or pain? How does that person comfort you?

Jesus gives us some very practical help in these verses for facing life's crises. He doesn't answer all our questions, but he gives us what we need to survive. *Read John 16:16-24.*

1. It is obvious that the disciples are confused and concerned about Jesus' statements (vv. 16-18). Why do you think they are so upset?

2. Jesus answers their questions not by giving them an explanation but by making them a promise (vv. 19-22). What is the promise?

Why would it bring them joy in the middle of their grief and
confusion?

3. How can this incident help us when our questions to the Lord
seemingly go unanswered?

4. What new promise regarding prayer does Jesus give his disciples
(vv. 23-24)?

5. How would that promise make their joy complete?

6. What connection can you make for your own life between
problems, prayer and joy?

7. *Read John 16:25-33.* How would Jesus' assurance of the Father's
love help the disciples in the days just ahead of them?

8. In verse 32 Jesus predicts that his disciples will abandon him. How will Jesus' promise of peace and victory (v. 33) sustain and help you after a time of failure?

9. Which of the promises in this chapter has made the deepest impression on you, and why?

10. How can you use these promises to strengthen a friend who is going through trials or discouragement?

 Give God whatever grief or sorrow you are carrying. Open yourself to the Spirit's peace.

NOW OR LATER

Both Jesus and the world offer a form of joy (John 15:11; 16:22-24), peace (John 14:27; 16:33) and love (John 13:34-35; 15:9-19). What is the difference between what the world offers and what Jesus offers?

How have you experienced both types of love, joy and peace?

EIGHT

JESUS PRAYS FOR US

John 17

I work as a chaplain for a hospice organization, and I talk with a lot of people who know they are near death. Sometimes we chat about their memories of life; more often we discuss the realities of the next life. The one thing I have noticed is that the approach of death has a way of bringing our priorities into very sharp focus. People who know death is imminent also know what is really important in life and who they really care about.

Group Discussion. Other than your relationship with the Lord, what two or three relationships are most valuable to you? What one thing would you ask God to do for each of those important people?

Personal Reflection. What goal do you want to reach before the end of your life? What are you doing today to help you reach that goal?

In Jesus' final prayer with his disciples, he prays for himself, for them and for you! Every believer is on Jesus' mind as he faces the greatest trial of his life—the cross. *Read John 17.*

1. Jesus makes only one request for himself—that the Father would glorify him so he might glorify the Father. Why do you think that was so important to Jesus?

2. To what extent is God's glory foremost in your mind on a daily basis? Explain your answer.

3. How is Jesus' definition of eternal life (v. 3) different from merely living forever?

4. According to verses 6-19, what specific ministries does Jesus have toward his disciples?

5. Twice Jesus asks the Father to protect his disciples from the evil one (vv. 11, 15). Why would that protection be so important in Jesus' mind as he faces the cross?

6. Jesus also asks the Father to sanctify his disciples through his Word (v. 17). How can we allow God's Word to have that kind of effect on our lives?

7. Jesus prays that those who believe in him would be one, "so that the world may believe that you have sent me" (vv. 21, 23). Why is our unity a powerful argument for the truth of Jesus' claims?

8. In what practical ways can we demonstrate our oneness with other believers?

9. Jesus obviously prays this prayer out loud to bring comfort and assurance to his disciples. How do Jesus' words encourage or assure you?

10. Jesus does not simply pray for the immediate, urgent needs of himself and his disciples. Instead he focuses on the long-range, important goals of their ministries. How are your prayers like or unlike Jesus' prayer?

 Express to God your sincere desire to glorify him in all you do.

NOW OR LATER

Construct your own prayer based on Jesus' model. Pray for yourself, the people closest to you and the people whom you influence in the workplace or neighborhood. What do you want God to accomplish long-range in each person? Now pray the prayer regularly. Refine it as God gives you direction. Watch God work!

NINE

TRIAL & TRUST

John 18:1-27

M ost of us can't imagine being arrested, imprisoned and brought to trial. If we were guilty of a crime, it would be humiliating. But if we were innocent, it would be devastating.

Group Discussion. How would you respond if someone falsely accused you of a crime and even called the police to have you arrested?

Personal Reflection. What would you do if someone betrayed your best friend?

In what should have been the most demeaning experience of his life, Jesus exhibits majesty and glory. Against a backdrop of attack, betrayal and abandonment, we see the brilliance of Christ's confident trust in the Father. His calm assurance will help us face life's hurts and injustices with the same trust in the same Father. *Read John 18:1-27.*

1. If you had been one of Jesus' disciples, what emotions would have gripped you when the soldiers arrived at the garden?

2. Why would Jesus go to a place where Judas knew he might be found (vv. 1-3)?

3. When the soldiers say they are seeking Jesus of Nazareth, Jesus replies "I am he" (v. 5). How would you explain the reaction of the soldiers (v. 6)?

4. What insight do Peter's action and Jesus' rebuke (v. 11) give you about your attempts to act out of your own strength and wisdom?

5. Think back to the deepest sin of your life. How does a look at your own sin change your attitude toward Peter's denial of Jesus?

6. If you had been in Peter's place, what reasons might you have given for denying that you were a disciple of Jesus?

7. When and where is it hardest for you to openly identify yourself as a Christian?

8. What can we learn from Peter's failure about being prepared to stand against the world's challenges?

9. John writes this account to highlight Jesus' courage, his power and his obedience to the Father. Which aspect of Jesus' character impresses you most?

10. What can you do to more clearly express your loyalty to Jesus when you are around other people?

 Admit any fear of identifying with Christ. Ask God to strengthen your faith to answer the world's challenges.

NOW OR LATER

Learn more about what Christian ministries are available to prisoners and their families in your community. Call the chaplain at your county jail or at a nearby state prison. Volunteer to help with a prison service. Pray for the moving of God's Spirit in the hearts of prisoners.

TEN

CHARACTER TEST

John 18:28–19:16

"C hrist killers!" The words made my stomach tighten. Someone had spray-painted the phrase and a series of swastikas on the Jewish synagogue in our city. Anti-Semitism had raised its ugly head again.

The New Testament writers certainly blame the Jewish leaders for condemning Jesus to die. But they didn't act alone. The Roman governor, Pontius Pilate, agreed to the death penalty. He did so even though he knew Jesus was innocent.

Group Discussion. To what extent are you tempted to compromise your Christian faith or witness because of pressure from people around you? Describe a situation in which you sensed that pressure.

Personal Reflection. Are you a person who stands for what is right, regardless of the consequences, or do you tend to compromise to keep the peace? When have you wished you were more the other way?

In the broader perspective of the plan of God, many people share the blame for Jesus' death. In a sense, all of us killed Jesus—he died for *our* sins and in *our* place. The most amazing answer to the question of who killed Jesus is that no one did! Jesus said, "No one takes my life from me. I lay it down of my own choice." *Read John 18:28-37.*

1. A Roman trial included four basic elements. What events or statements from John's account fall under each category?

| The accusation:

| The interrogation or search for evidence:

| The defense:

| The verdict:

| **2.** How do the Jewish leaders reveal their hypocrisy by refusing to enter Pilate's (a non-Jewish) home (v. 28)?

| **3.** How would you describe Jesus' "kingdom" based on his response to Pilate (vv. 36-37)?

| **4.** *Read John 18:38–19:16.* Pilate obviously is trying to release Jesus. What specific attempts does he make?

| **5.** How does it make you feel when you read the record of injustice done toward Jesus?

6. What can you conclude about Pilate's character after reading this passage?

7. The Jews' true charge against Jesus comes out in verse 7: "He claimed to be the Son of God." Why do you think Pilate reacts to that statement the way he does (19:8-9)?

8. Why doesn't Jesus say more to Pilate and defend himself more vigorously (19:9-11)?

9. What would you have done if you had been Pilate?

10. What does this passage teach you about how to respond when you are treated unjustly?

Ask Jesus, who faced Pilate's injustice with courage and grace, to give you the strength to stand firmly for what is right and good.

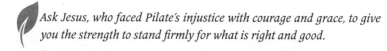

NOW OR LATER

In the middle of a degrading experience, Jesus is portrayed as a King. Who or what are some of the "kings" people obey today?

Who or what competes with Christ for authority over your life?

ELEVEN

OBEDIENT
TO DEATH

John 19:17-42

T here is nothing pleasant or attractive about an execution. The only one I've ever seen was in a televised news report from Vietnam. A captured soldier was shot. It left a knot in my stomach for days.

Group Discussion. Tell about how a national or international assassination affected you and how you learned about the tragedy.

Personal Reflection. When you think about death, what feelings and thoughts come to mind?

In Jesus' day execution was designed to be public and painful. The account of the crucifixion is not easy to read. You may be tempted to think that Jesus' death was a cruel mistake. It wasn't. Jesus' life was not taken from him; he laid it down willingly. His cross was, in a very real sense, our cross. *Read John 19:17-42.*

1. Crucifixion was obviously a brutal and tortuous form of execution. Why do you think John leaves so much of the agonizing detail out of his account?

2. Three groups are involved in Jesus' death—the soldiers, the Jewish leaders and Pilate. How would you characterize each one's attitude toward Jesus?

3. In what ways do their attitudes toward Jesus parallel those of men and women today?

4. How do you think Mary, Jesus' mother, feels as she stands by the cross?

5. How is Jesus' tender care for her evident even while he is dying (vv. 26-27)?

6. What is the significance of Jesus' cry, "It is finished" (v. 30; see John 17:4)?

7. What feelings and thoughts would have gone through your mind if you had helped prepare Jesus' body for burial?

8. Where are Jesus' disciples during his crucifixion and burial (see John 16:32)?

Why do you think they are so conspicuously absent?

9. Under the same circumstances, do you think you would have been more like Joseph and Nicodemus or Jesus' disciples? Explain your answer.

10. When it comes to public identification with Jesus, how is it possible to respond in the same ways today?

11. What aspect of Jesus' death has made the deepest impression on you and why?

 Thank Jesus for enduring the cross so that you could be forgiven and restored to a right relationship with God.

NOW OR LATER

Some critics of the Bible claim that Jesus never really died on the cross. What evidence does John provide that refutes that view? Why was it so important for John to establish the certainty of Jesus' death?

TWELVE

THE SON IS UP!

John 20

The story circulated for days in the hospital where my brother worked. An orderly was told to take a body to the morgue. Simply out of habit, the orderly felt the man's wrist for a pulse. When he realized his mistake, the orderly quickly dropped the arm, but not before his sensitive fingers told him something his mind struggled to believe. There was a pulse! The doctors were called, and the man was revived.

Group Discussion. How would you react if a friend told you he had seen someone raised from the dead?

Personal Reflection. Why is it important to you that Jesus rose from the dead? Could you still believe in him if he had died and we could visit his tomb?

The hospital story my brother told me may or may not be fully accurate. But I know of one account of a man coming back to life that is true. The man lived for years after the event. In fact, he is still alive! *Read John 20.*

1. John identifies three witnesses to the empty tomb: Mary Magdalene, Peter and "the other disciple" (John himself). What important details do we learn from each one (vv. 1-9)?

2. Why is it important to prove the tomb was empty?

3. John also records three appearances of the risen Christ: to Mary Magdalene, to his disciples and to Thomas. Why do you think Mary Magdalene doesn't immediately recognize Jesus (vv. 10-15)?

After she does recognize him, what impresses you most about their encounter (vv. 16-18)?

4. When Jesus appears to his disciples, what specific gifts and promises does he give them (vv. 19-23)?

What do you think is the significance of each gift or promise?

5. Finally, Jesus appears to Thomas (vv. 24-29). How does Thomas's attitude—both before and after Jesus appears to him—add credibility to the resurrection?

6. How does Thomas's exclamation "My Lord and my God" (v. 28) provide a fitting climax to John's Gospel?

7. What can we learn from Jesus' encounter with Thomas about helping people who have doubts about the Christian message?

8. On what evidence do you base your belief that Jesus rose from the dead?

9. Is believing that Jesus rose from the dead as important as believing that he died on the cross for our sins? Explain why or why not.

10. John tells us why he has written his Gospel in verses 30 and 31. Of all the "miraculous signs" John has included, which have been most convincing to you, and why?

 Praise Jesus as your risen Savior. Use Thomas's words, "My Lord and my God," as you address Jesus.

NOW OR LATER

Mary Magdalene wanted to hold on to Jesus, but Jesus sent her on a mission to tell others that he was alive. Who is someone you can tell about Jesus and his resurrection? Make a plan to talk with that person this week. Ask God to give you an opportunity to share the message.

THIRTEEN

A WALK WITH
A RESURRECTED MAN

John 21

M ost of us find it easier to forgive than to forget. We may be
ready to forgive someone who has hurt us deeply, but we have
a hard time trusting that person again.

Group Discussion. Tell the group about a broken relationship you tried
to restore and what resulted from your effort.

Personal Reflection. Describe how you feel when someone you have
hurt refuses to forgive you.

Peter failed Jesus miserably. He promised to give up his life if necessary
to protect Jesus but then denied even knowing him a few hours later.
Peter knew Jesus had forgiven him. The question that pressed on Peter's
heart was, Would Jesus trust him again? Could Jesus still use him to
bring glory to God? *Read John 21:1-14.*

1. What is the significance of Peter's decision to return to fishing
(vv. 1-3)?

2. What is Jesus trying to show the disciples by allowing them to
catch such a large number of fish (vv. 4-6; see Luke 5:4-11)?

3. When Peter hears that "it is the Lord" (vv. 7-8), he jumps into the water and begins swimming ahead of the boat. What does that response reveal about Peter and his relationship with Jesus?

4. How would you have responded if you had denied Jesus just a few days earlier?

5. *Read John 21:15-25.* What subtle differences do you notice in Jesus' three questions and Peter's responses (vv. 15-17)?

What do you think is the significance of those differences?

6. What can we learn from this passage about the steps involved in restoring a Christian who has sinned?

7. Why do you think Jesus chooses this particular occasion to predict the kind of death Peter would die (vv. 18-19)?

8. How does it help to know that you can still serve and glorify God no matter what your past failures have been?

9. What does Jesus' rebuke to Peter (v. 22) reveal about the danger of comparing ourselves with other Christians?

10. Picture Jesus saying these things to you. How would you respond, or what would the words mean in the context of your life?

"Do you truly love me?"

"Take care of my sheep."

"You must follow me."

 Express your willingness to do whatever Jesus asks you to do.

NOW OR LATER

As you have studied John's Gospel, what aspects of Jesus' character or ministry have impressed you most?

What responses have you made in your heart and life as a result of that deeper understanding?

LEADER'S NOTES

My grace is sufficient for you.

2 CORINTHIANS 12:9

Leading a Bible discussion can be an enjoyable and rewarding experience. But it can also be *scary*—especially if you've never done it before. If this is your feeling, you're in good company. When God asked Moses to lead the Israelites out of Egypt, he replied, "O Lord, please send someone else to do it"! (Ex 4:13). It was the same with Solomon, Jeremiah and Timothy, but God helped these people in spite of their weaknesses, and he will help you as well.

You don't need to be an expert on the Bible or a trained teacher to lead a Bible discussion. The idea behind these inductive studies is that the leader guides group members to discover for themselves what the Bible has to say. This method of learning will allow group members to remember much more of what is said than a lecture would.

These studies are designed to be led easily. As a matter of fact, the flow of questions through the passage from observation to interpretation to application is so natural that you may feel that the studies lead themselves. This study guide is also flexible. You can use it with a variety of groups—student, professional, neighborhood or church groups. Each study takes forty-five to sixty minutes in a group setting.

There are some important facts to know about group dynamics and encouraging discussion. The suggestions listed below should enable you to effectively and enjoyably fulfill your role as leader.

PREPARING FOR THE STUDY

1. Ask God to help you understand and apply the passage in your own life. Unless this happens, you will not be prepared to lead others. Pray too for the various members of the group. Ask God to open your hearts to the message of his Word and motivate you to action.

2. Read the introduction to the entire guide to get an overview of the entire book and the issues which will be explored.

3. As you begin each study, read and reread the assigned Bible passage to familiarize yourself with it.

4. This study guide is based on the New International Version of the Bible. It will help you and the group if you use this translation as the basis for your study and discussion.

5. Carefully work through each question in the study. Spend time in meditation and reflection as you consider how to respond.

6. Write your thoughts and responses in the space provided in the study guide. This will help you to express your understanding of the passage clearly.

7. It might help to have a Bible dictionary handy. Use it to look up any unfamiliar words, names or places. (For additional help on how to study a passage, see chapter five of *Leading Bible Discussions,* Inter-Varsity Press.)

8. Consider how you can apply the Scripture to your life. Remember that the group will follow your lead in responding to the studies. They will not go any deeper than you do.

9. Once you have finished your own study of the passage, familiarize yourself with the leader's notes for the study you are leading. These are designed to help you in several ways. First, they tell you the purpose the study guide author had in mind when writing the study. Take time to think through how the study questions work together to accomplish that purpose. Second, the notes provide you with additional back-ground information or suggestions on group dynamics for various questions. This information can be useful when people have difficulty understanding or answering a question. Third, the leader's notes can alert you to potential problems you may encounter during the study.

10. If you wish to remind yourself of anything mentioned in the leader's notes, make a note to yourself below that question in the study.

LEADING THE STUDY

1. Begin the study on time. Open with prayer, asking God to help the group to understand and apply the passage.

2. Be sure that everyone in your group has a study guide. Encourage the group to prepare beforehand for each discussion by reading the introduction to the guide and by working through the questions in the study. **3.** At the beginning of your first time together, explain that these studies are meant to be discussions, not lectures. Encourage the members of the group to participate. However, do not put pressure on those who may be hesitant to speak during the first few sessions. You may want to suggest the following guidelines to your group.

- Stick to the topic being discussed.

- Your responses should be based on the verses which are the focus of the discussion and not on outside authorities such as commentaries or speakers.

- These studies focus on a particular passage of Scripture. Only rarely should you refer to other portions of the Bible. This allows for everyone to participate in in-depth study on equal ground.

- Anything said in the group is considered confidential and will not be discussed outside the group unless specific permission is given to do so.

- We will listen attentively to each other and provide time for each person present to talk.

- We will pray for each other.

4. Have a group member read the introduction at the beginning of the discussion.

5. Every session begins with a group discussion question. The question or activity is meant to be used before the passage is read. The question introduces the theme of the study and encourages group members to begin to open up. Encourage as many members as possible to participate, and be ready to get the discussion going with your own response.

This section is designed to reveal where our thoughts or feelings need to be transformed by Scripture. That is why it is especially important not to read the passage before the discussion question is asked. The passage will tend to color the honest reactions people would otherwise give because they are, of course, supposed to think the way the Bible does.

You may want to supplement the group discussion question with an icebreaker to help people to get comfortable. See the community section of *Small Group Idea Book* for more ideas. You also might want to use the personal reflection question with your group. Either allow a time of silence for people to respond individually or discuss it together.

6. Have a group member (or members if the passage is long) read aloud the passage to be studied. Then give people several minutes to read the passage again silently so that they can take it all in.

7. Question 1 will generally be an overview question designed to briefly survey the passage. Encourage the group to look at the whole passage, but try to avoid getting sidetracked by questions or issues that will be addressed later in the study.

8. As you ask the questions, keep in mind that they are designed to be used just as they are written. You may simply read them aloud. Or you may prefer to express them in your own words.

There may be times when it is appropriate to deviate from the study guide. For example, a question may have already been answered. If so, move on to the next question. Or someone may raise an important question not covered in the guide. Take time to discuss it, but try to keep the group from going off on tangents.

9. Avoid answering your own questions. If necessary, repeat or rephrase them until they are clearly understood. Or point out something you read in the leader's notes to clarify the context or meaning. An eager group quickly becomes passive and silent if they think the leader will do most of the talking.

10. Don't be afraid of silence. People may need time to think about the question before formulating their answers.

11. Don't be content with just one answer. Ask, "What do the rest of you think?" or "Anything else?" until several people have given answers to the question.

12. Acknowledge all contributions. Try to be affirming whenever possible. Never reject an answer. If it is clearly off-base, ask, "Which verse led you to that conclusion?" or again, "What do the rest of you think?"

13. Don't expect every answer to be addressed to you, even though this will probably happen at first. As group members become more at ease, they will begin to truly interact with each other. This is one sign of healthy discussion.

14. Don't be afraid of controversy. It can be very stimulating. If you don't resolve an issue completely, don't be frustrated. Move on and keep it in mind for later. A subsequent study may solve the problem.

15. Periodically summarize what the group has said about the passage. This helps to draw together the various ideas mentioned and gives continuity to the study. But don't preach.

16. At the end of the Bible discussion you may want to allow group members a time of quiet to work on an idea under "Now or Later." Then discuss what you experienced. Or you may want to encourage group members to work on these ideas between meetings. Give an opportunity during the session for people to talk about what they are learning.

17. Conclude your time together with conversational prayer, adapting the prayer suggestion at the end of the study to your group. Ask for God's help in following through on the commitments you've made.

18. End on time.

Many more suggestions and helps are found in *Leading Bible Discussions*, which is part of the LifeGuide Bible Study series.

COMPONENTS OF SMALL GROUPS

A healthy small group should do more than study the Bible. There are four components to consider as you structure your time together.

Nurture. Small groups help us to grow in our knowledge and love of God. Bible study is the key to making this happen and is the foundation of your small group.

Community. Small groups are a great place to develop deep friendships with other Christians. Allow time for informal interaction before and after each study. Plan activities and games that will help you get to know each other. Spend time having fun together—going on a picnic or cooking dinner together.

Worship and prayer. Your study will be enhanced by spending time praising God together in prayer or song. Pray for each other's needs— and keep track of how God is answering prayer in your group. Ask God to help you to apply what you are learning in your study.

Outreach. Reaching out to others can be a practical way of applying what you are learning, and it will keep your group from becoming self-focused. Host a series of evangelistic discussions for your friends or neighbors. Clean up the yard of an elderly friend. Serve at a soup kitchen together, or spend a day working on a Habitat house.

Many more suggestions and helps in each of these areas are found in *Small Group Idea Book.* Information on building a small group can be found in *Small Group Leaders' Handbook* and *The Big Book on Small Groups* (both from InterVarsity Press). Reading through one of these books would be worth your time.

Almost every statement I have made about the Gospel of John in the introduction to the study guide has been challenged by some New Testament scholar! I have written from the position held by most evangelical students of John's Gospel. As group leader it might be helpful for you to read a conservative introduction to the Gospel. The standard work (both introduction and commentary) is by Leon Morris (*The Gospel According to John,* New International Commentaries on the New Testament [Grand Rapids, Mich.: Eerdmans, 1971]). It is a scholarly study but filled with insight and devotion to Christ.

Other good sources are

Bruce Milne, *The Message of John,* The Bible Speaks Today (Downers Grove, Ill.: InterVarsity Press, 1993).

Gary Burge, *John,* NIV Application Commentary (Grand Rapids, Mich.: Zondervan, 1999).

One profitable way to introduce your group to John's Gospel is to compare the four Gospels in regard to their authorship, audience, purpose and message. In that way you can emphasize John's unique contribution to our understanding of Jesus Christ. Any Bible handbook will give you help in putting together such a comparison. More information is available on the page for this study guide at the IVP website ivpress.com.

STUDY 1. JOHN 13:1-17. THE SON AS A SLAVE.

PURPOSE: To impress us with Jesus' example of loving servanthood and to motivate us to display the same spirit.

Question 1. These verses set the scene for Jesus' entire farewell message to his disciples. Jesus knew that the hour had come for the completion of his mission on earth. In that light he wanted to demonstrate the full range of his love for his disciples.

Question 2. The famous portrayals of the Last Supper by artists are almost all incorrect. Jesus and his disciples were not sitting on chairs at a table. They were reclining on low couches arranged (most likely) around low tables in a "U" shape. Jesus, as the guest of honor, reclined in the center position. John reclined on Jesus' right; Judas reclined on Jesus' left. Both men had places of honor next to Jesus, places Jesus had invited them to occupy.

Question 3. When people entered a house, it was customary to wash their feet. A water pot stood outside the door, and usually a slave was stationed there to perform the task. Often the job was given to a disabled or mentally challenged slave who couldn't do anything else. If there was no slave at the door, one of the members of the group would wash the feet of the others out of courtesy. But on the day Jesus and his disciples came to the upper room, no one volunteered.

The "upper room" was a large room in a house that was used for large family gatherings. It was probably built as a second story over the family dwelling below. Visitors had access by way of an outside staircase. Jesus and his disciples had borrowed the room of a friend for this last "family" gathering before Jesus' death.

Question 7. Peter's unwillingness to have his feet washed was a response that characterized Jesus' enemies. But the other extreme ("wash me all over") missed the point too. Peter did not need to be rebathed (reborn); he needed only a cleansing from daily sin.

Question 8. Some Christians regularly practice footwashing as part of their worship. Other Christians do not because the practice is never commanded to the church in the later New Testament. Certainly the spirit of servanthood is to characterize every Christian's life. If your group is open to the idea, you may want to conclude your study time with your own footwashing service. Provide basins of water and towels, and have each person rinse the feet of the person next to them. Usually words of encouragement and love are spoken after each person's feet are washed. It can be a very moving experience but also one that stretches some people beyond their comfort zone.

STUDY 2. JOHN 13:18-38. A TRAITOR? NOT ME!

PURPOSE: To teach us to look beyond surface appearance to genuine character when choosing our spiritual heroes.

Question 2. Judas's impending betrayal came as no surprise to Jesus (see Jn 6:66-71). Jesus knew Judas's intention, of course, and yet Jesus continued to minister to Judas in exactly the same way he ministered to his other disciples. No one knew from Jesus' attitude that Judas was the betrayer.

Judas reclined at Jesus' left; John reclined at Jesus' right. John could easily lean back on Jesus and engage in intimate conversation that the other disciples may not have heard or understood. Jesus could also talk quietly with Judas without attracting undue attention. To dip bread in a dish of chopped fruit and give it to another person at the table was an act of friendship. It is comparable to proposing a toast in our culture. Jesus used the gesture to continue to reach out to Judas in love.

You may also want to discuss the statement in verse 27: "Satan entered into him." Judas is the only person described in Scripture as being personally indwelt by Satan. Consider why John would make this point.

Question 5. The new covenant that Jesus made with his disciples had just one commandment (not ten commandments like the old covenant). Jesus' command was to love each other—to make a choice to act for the good of your brothers and sisters in Christ, to love them regardless of their response to you, to keep on loving even when they are unlovely or unlovable.

Question 7. Love is to be the mark of Jesus' disciples. When people around see the sacrificial love we have for each other, they will immediately recognize that we follow Jesus. Compare that quality with other qualities that Christians sometimes think will gain the world's attention—knowledge or miraculous works or political influence.

Question 8. Peter speaks from an exaggerated confidence in his own ability. Peter would follow Jesus in death later on (see Jn 21:19), but Peter wanted to follow Jesus now.

STUDY 3. JOHN 14. COMFORT FOR A TROUBLED HEART.

PURPOSE: To understand and claim the comfort available to us in Christ and in his promises.

Question 1. Jesus had revealed that one of his disciples would betray him, that he would be leaving and the disciples could not follow, and that Peter would disown Jesus that very night—troubling words!

Question 3. Thomas and Philip had not fully grasped the fact that Jesus was God in visible form.

Question 4. Those who think Christians are "too narrow" in their belief that Jesus is the only way to God need to be reminded that we are only agreeing with what Jesus himself said. It should also be noted that Jesus did not say, "The church is the way," or "Christianity is the way." He said, "*I* am the way."

Question 5. This chapter contains the first of several sections in John's Gospel on the ministry of the Holy Spirit. If you are unfamiliar with the teaching of the New Testament on the Spirit and his work, it would be profitable to do some reading in a theological work that addresses this important area.

Question 7. Our obedience to Christ emerges from our love for him. We are not motivated to obey Christ by the law (I *must* do this); we are motivated by love (I *want* to do this).

Question 8. The peace Jesus brings is an inner work of the Holy Spirit. It is not dependent on outside circumstances or events. Jesus' peace is a sense of security and safety in his love. The world's peace is simply the absence of conflict. A person of the world can have an abundance of wealth and be in turmoil; a Christian can be in a prison cell or a hospital bed and be at peace.

STUDY 4. JOHN 15:1-11. THE SECRET OF THE VINE.

PURPOSE: To challenge us to seek a deeper level of commitment to spiritual intimacy with the Lord Jesus.

Question 1. The vine is used in the Old Testament as a figure for the people of Israel as God's chosen people (see Ps 80:8-19). But the psalmist also foresees the coming of a divine Redeemer—"the man at your right hand, the son of man you have raised up for yourself." Jesus was the *true* vine, the unfailing channel of God's grace and power.

Question 2. This is a good place in the study to insert the necessity of being a "branch" (a Christian). No one shares in Christ's life unless there is a faith relationship to Jesus.

Question 3. *Remain* means to be joined to and to stay in that relationship. By remaining in the vine, the branch draws its nourishment and life from the vine. Believers who remain in union with Christ learn to draw their strength, spiritual resources, life and joy from him. Jesus is talking about more than a casual, once-a-week relationship; he's talking about an ongoing, deepening relationship.

Question 4. Several elements maintain our relationship with Christ: prayer, reading and meditating on the Word, worship alone and in community, obedience to the Spirit, a joyful desire to grow.

Question 5. Fruit in the New Testament is the observable evidence of our true inner nature. If we are branches connected to Jesus the vine, we should demonstrate Christlike qualities in our lives. Paul calls those outward qualities the "fruit of the Spirit" (Gal 5:22-23).

Question 6. A number of views exist on what it means for a branch to be "cut off." One is that the Christian who refuses to grow and bear fruit makes a choice to reject his or her place in Christ. A second view is that this is a reference to God's discipline in the life of an unproductive Christian. The genuine believer does not become separated from Christ but is reproved by God. A third view is that the unproductive branches were not genuine believers in the first place.

If a number of views are represented by members of your study group, give time for a presentation of each view, but don't let this issue overshadow the rest of the biblical teaching. If everyone in the group seems to hold to one view, you may want to challenge that view to test the depth of conviction in the other members.

Question 8. The Holy Spirit will continue to testify to who Jesus was and to what Jesus accomplished. The disciples will also bear that responsibility as eyewitnesses of Jesus' life, death and resurrection. These two sources provide the testimony that still persuades people today to believe on Jesus—the testimony of the New Testament and the inner convincing power of the Holy Spirit.

STUDY 5. JOHN 15:12-16:4. THE COST OF FRIENDSHIP.

PURPOSE: To explore the personal relationship that Jesus desires to have with us and to use that relationship as a model for our relationships with others.

Question 2. We use the term *friend* in a much more casual way than the people in Jesus' day used it. For them, friendship included loyalty, equality, the sharing of possessions and even the sharing of secrets. The word Jesus uses here in Greek means someone who is part of the king's inner circle.

Question 5. Jesus had been (and would continue to be) the target of hostility. Once Jesus was off the scene, however, the world's hatred would be directed toward his followers. The response of the unbelieving world to Christians mirrors their response to Jesus.

Question 6. The hostility of the world is the price the believer pays for friendship with Christ. You need to draw the distinction between persecution for Christ's sake or persecution that comes because we do something personally offensive.

Question 7. Jesus had given his generation enough evidence to prove his claim to be God. They heard his words and saw his miracles, but they rejected him anyway. Therefore, they were guilty of rejecting God and had no excuse for their sin.

STUDY 6. JOHN 16:5-15. SECRETS OF THE SPIRIT.

PURPOSE: To realize the power of the Holy Spirit that is available to us as we face the struggles and problems of life.

Question 2. The Counselor mentioned in verse 7 is obviously the Holy Spirit (see 15:26; 16:13-15).

Verse 5 seems to be a contradiction. Someone *did* ask Jesus where he was going. Back in John 13:36, Peter said, "Lord, where are you going?" Peter, however, was not concerned about Jesus' destination but about being separated from him. Instead of rejoicing because Jesus was going to the Father, he was sorrowful about being left alone.

Question 3. The Holy Spirit is fully present in every true believer in Christ. On earth Jesus limited himself to a human body and could only be at one place at any one time. Every believer has personal, direct access to God through the Holy Spirit. If Jesus were here, we would have to wait in line to have personal, direct access to God.

Question 4. The Spirit's work toward the world is to "convict" the world of several important things. The word translated "convict" means to present evidence so as to convince. Those who hear the gospel are convinced by the Holy Spirit of certain facts about themselves and about Jesus. Even those who reject the gospel are convinced of its truth. Their rejection is a matter of the will. They deliberately choose to reject what they have been convinced is true.

Question 6. Jesus' death on the cross and his resurrection from the dead sealed Satan's ultimate condemnation. Satan is still active in our world, but he is a defeated enemy.

Question 8. God has given Christians the responsibility of communicating the gospel message. It is the Holy Spirit's responsibility to convince those who hear the message of its truth.

Question 9. The end result of the Spirit's work of communication to the disciples is the written New Testament. The apostles' written testimony about Jesus is the foundation on which we rest our faith (see Eph 2:19-20).

Question 10. The Spirit is not revealing new Scripture to us today. His ministry is to illumine our minds to understand what is already written and to apply that truth to our contemporary culture.

STUDY 7. JOHN 7:16-33. PEACE IN A TIME OF TROUBLE.

PURPOSE: To equip us to handle crisis situations for which we have no explanation or answers.

General note. This section is especially conducive to open sharing of struggles, fears and failures. You may not have answers to the problems that emerge from the group. The focus of the study is that, even in the times of greatest darkness and confusion, we have not been abandoned. We can still cling to the Father's love and the Spirit's presence. It might be profitable to end the study with specific prayer for the people and the needs in the group.

Question 1. The disciples were confused by the prospect of Jesus' departure and then return—and by the timing of those events. They had already heard some very disturbing things and now Jesus adds more to be concerned about.

Question 3. We have questions: What is going on? Why is this happening? When will it end? When they go unanswered, we can be certain that God is at work and will ultimately bring joy out of a difficult and desperate situation.

Question 5. The disciples would find new confidence in prayer. They could now come to the Father in Jesus' name—in his place, in his authority. Whenever we pray for what Jesus would pray for in the same situation, the Father will give it to us. The question "What would Jesus do?" has been overworked, but maybe we need to ask "What would Jesus pray for?"

Question 7. As the disciples hid in fear after Jesus' crucifixion, they must have thought back often to Jesus' assurance of the Father's love.

Question 8. We don't find peace in sin or disobedience, but after we return to the Lord we find peace in his forgiveness and love.

STUDY 8. JOHN 17. JESUS PRAYS FOR US.

PURPOSE: To reveal the concerns of Jesus' heart as he faced the cross and to see how those concerns should be our concerns as his followers.

Question 1. Jesus' primary goal in coming to earth was not directed at human beings but at God the Father. He came to reveal how good and gracious the Father is to provide a way for disobedient humanity to be restored to a right relationship with him. This is a theme all through John's Gospel. Jesus came to do the Father's will (4:34; 5:30, 38; 6:38-39) and the Father's work (5:36; 9:4). He also came to speak the Father's words (3:34; 7:16; 12:49), to bear witness to the Father (5:36; 7:28) and to live in a close relationship with the Father (8:16, 18, 29; 16:32). Christians are to follow Jesus' example in pursuing God's glory (17:18; 20:21).

Question 3. The phrase "eternal life" refers to a kind of life, not just a length of time. Eternal life begins when a person enters a relationship with God through faith in Jesus Christ (Jn 3:36; 5:24). At that moment we have a whole new kind of life—God's life, eternal life.

Question 5. The crucifixion and death of Jesus would look for a while like Jesus' defeat and Satan's victory. The enemy would use that time of confusion to push the disciples toward despair, disbelief or even suicide. Jesus asked the Father to protect the disciples during that particularly vulnerable time. A follow-up question might be, "Is that the kind of protection we can still ask God for?"

Question 6. The word *sanctify* means to set apart. In Scripture it has a double thrust—to be set apart from sin and to be set apart for God's use. Explore both themes in your discussion.

Question 7. The tendency is to read organizational unity into Jesus' prayer instead of organic unity. It might be profitable to review the "unity" pictures Jesus has already used: one flock (Jn 10) and Jesus as the vine and believers as the branches (Jn 15).

STUDY 9. JOHN 18:1-27. TRIAL & TRUST.

PURPOSE: To show Jesus' sovereign control and calm confidence in a time of trial, and to give us assurance in our difficult times.

Question 1. The obvious emotion is fear. But explore other struggles the disciples must have faced. What would they have felt toward Judas? What about their promises to die with Jesus?

Question 2. Jesus wanted to make it easy for Judas to find him and for the soldiers to arrest him without incident. The olive grove was also a place where the disciples could escape easily into the night. John portrays Jesus always as the victor, never as the victim. Jesus orchestrates the whole scene.

Question 3. Jesus spoke a simple word of response: "I am." That was the name the Lord spoke to Moses from the burning bush in Exodus 3:14. Jesus attributed to himself the personal name of the Lord God.

Question 4. Jesus establishes that the soldiers are seeking only him, yet Peter steps outside Jesus' protection in a feeble attempt to fight off the entire group. Our attempts at working things out sometimes complicate what God has already planned and put into place for our good.

Question 6. Peter realized the seriousness of Jesus' situation. Another cross could quickly be found for him! Despite his noble intentions, Peter's faith was too weak to stand up to this challenge at this point in his life.

It might be helpful to outline the main events of Jesus' trials in sequence for the group. A study Bible or a book on the life of Christ should provide you with those details.

Two men are called the "high priest" in John 18—Caiaphas in verse 12 and Annas in verse 19. Annas was the legitimate high priest of Israel under Jewish law. Some years earlier, however, the Roman authorities decided to sell the office to the highest bidder. Annas proceeded to buy the position for a whole succession of men. Caiaphas, the high priest that year, was Annas's son-in-law. Because Annas was the real power behind the office, the Jewish leaders took Jesus to Annas first.

The other disciple mentioned in verse 15 has generally been identified as John, the author of this Gospel. John may have been from a priestly family and would, therefore, have been known to the high priest.

Question 8. Peter probably entered the temple complex thinking he would try to get close to Jesus and somehow set him free. What Peter wasn't expecting was a challenge from a servant girl. Once in the "denial" mode, it became more and more difficult to admit his true allegiance. **Question 10.** The suggestions shared in answer to this question need to be "tested" by the response of others in the group. Sometimes our attempts to "stand for Christ" are really expressions of pride or self-righteousness. How did Jesus act in front of others when he was questioned?

STUDY 10. JOHN 18:28-19:16. CHARACTER TEST.

PURPOSE: To demonstrate that even though Jesus was crucified unjustly, he willingly submitted to death for our sins.

General note. Pontius Pilate was a Roman career bureaucrat about the same age as Jesus. His official title was procurator of Judea. He came to Judea in A.D. 26, hoping that he would soon be promoted to a more civilized section of the empire. From the moment he arrived in Judea, however, everything went wrong. After two or three major political blunders, Pilate found himself at the mercy of the Jewish leaders. They knew that enough pressure would make Pilate do whatever they asked.

Jesus' final religious trial had been held in the temple area in the chamber of the Sanhedrin (san-heed-rin), the Jewish supreme court. Right next to the temple was the Roman fortress of Antonia. The Roman army was stationed there, and Pilate, the governor, lived there. So it required just a short walk to bring Jesus to the civil authority for final condemnation.

Question 2. While about to execute an innocent man, the Jewish leaders are scrupulously concerned about avoiding ceremonial contamination during Passover. They refuse to enter Pilate's house for fear of coming in contact with something or someone unclean.

Since the Sanhedrin, the Jewish council, did not have the authority legally to impose the death sentence, they needed the sanction of Rome to have Jesus executed. John also recognizes that a Roman style of death was necessary so that Jesus' words about the manner of his death (being "lifted up") would be fulfilled (v. 32). The penalty under Jewish law for blasphemy was stoning.

Question 3. Jesus' kingdom did not originate within the world system. Its principles of operation are very different from the kingdom Pilate represented. You may want to discuss some of the differences.

Question 4. Pilate repeatedly said that he found nothing in Jesus' actions or words that warranted death. Pilate tried to play on Jesus' popularity with the crowd to get Jesus released, but to Pilate's shock the crowd called for Barabbas to be released, not Jesus. Then Pilate tried sympathy. Jesus was whipped and presented back to the crowd. But they still called for his death.

The flogging mentioned in 19:1 was no light punishment. The whip had pieces of metal or glass embedded in the leather thongs. The beating ripped open the flesh not only on a person's back but also on his chest and face. Jesus would have been almost unrecognizable after the ordeal.

Question 7. Roman mythology was full of characters born from a union of the gods with mortals. Was Jesus a son of one of the gods? The thought brought panic to Pilate's pagan mind.

Question 8. Isaiah, the Old Testament prophet, said that the Messiah would face execution as a "lamb to the slaughter" (Is 53:7-8). Jesus spoke to Pilate only to confront Pilate with his own need and the injustice of his condemnation. Later church historians claim that Pilate eventually committed suicide after being recalled to Rome and exiled to Gaul (modern France).

Question 9. Try to get beyond the superficial responses and help those in the group realize that we probably would have caved in to political pressure just like Pilate did.

STUDY 11. JOHN 19:17-42. OBEDIENT TO DEATH.

PURPOSE: To grasp the incredible price Jesus paid for our redemption from sin.

Question 1. A fascinating article on the crucifixion of Jesus was published in 1986 by a medical doctor, a pastor and a graphic artist. If you wish to obtain a copy for your own research or for the group, the article is titled "On the Physical Death of Jesus Christ" by William D. Edwards,

Wesley Gabel and Floyd Hosmer, *The Journal of the American Medical Association* 255 (March 21, 1986): 1455-63.

Question 4. Very few of Jesus' followers were brave enough to identify with him at his execution. John mentions only five: Jesus' mother, Mary; his aunt, Salome, the mother of John (who wrote this Gospel); Mary, the wife of Clopas; Mary Magdalene; and John, the author. Although Jesus was occupied with the most important event in the history of redemption, he remembered to care for the needs of his mother. Usually younger brothers were entrusted with a widowed mother's care but Jesus' brothers at this point were not believers. Jesus placed Mary in the care of his cousin, John.

Question 6. Jesus spoke on seven occasions during the six hours on the cross. John records three incidents. His cry, "It is finished," was a declaration of victory; the full payment for our sins had been made. The word Jesus spoke in Greek meant a debt had been paid in full. Nothing else needs to be or can be added to our redemption. Those who believe in Jesus are under no further obligation before God. We walk in obedience to God out of love for him and out of gratitude for what he has done, not because we add anything to our salvation by good works.

Question 7. The bodies of crucified criminals were normally thrown down the side of Golgotha into the valley of Hinnom, Jerusalem's garbage dump, where they were devoured by scavenging animals. Joseph of Arimathea and Nicodemus (the same man we met in Jn 3) had enough clout and money to get permission to take Jesus' body and bury it. A few of Jesus' followers washed his body and quickly wrapped it with strips of linen held in place by gummy spices. Since the next day was a special holy day for the Jews, no bodies were left hanging on crosses overnight.

Now or Later. John had to verify Jesus' actual death in order to substantiate a genuine resurrection in chapter 20. Every witness affirmed that Jesus was dead—John himself (v. 26), the executioners and Jesus' friends who took his body away.

The legs of the victim were broken in order to speed his death. Survival on the cross required the victim to push up with his legs so that his lungs could fill with air. Hanging from his hands produced paralysis in the diaphragm. Only the constant and painful up-and-down movement allowed the man to live. When his legs were broken, he could no longer push up and, as a result, died in a few minutes. A victim of crucifixion did not die from loss of blood but from suffocation.

The blood and water that flowed from the spear wound in Jesus' side (v. 34) was another evidence of his death. The blood in the heart had already separated. The heavier red blood cells had separated from the plasma, the clear liquid John called "water." John records this observation as another proof that Jesus actually died. Modern theories that Jesus swooned or fainted on the cross and later revived have no support in the facts recorded for us by eyewitnesses.

STUDY 12. JOHN 20. THE SON IS UP!

PURPOSE: To affirm the reality of the resurrection of Jesus, and to show how we can respond to people who doubt or disbelieve.

Question 1. The position of the burial wrappings (vv. 6-7) is a significant piece of evidence. Jewish burial practice involved wrapping the washed body in strips of linen from the shoulders to the toes. As the wrapping was done, a mixture of gummy spices was spread on the cloth to hold the binding and to cover the stench of decay. A large square of linen cloth was wrapped over the head and face and was tied under the jaw.

When Peter and John entered the tomb, they saw the linen burial cocoon still in place, but the body was gone. The cloth that had been around Jesus' head was in its place by itself. The resurrection body of Jesus had passed through the burial wrappings, and they had collapsed in place.

Question 2. Jesus' resurrection was not just a "spiritual" experience in which Jesus continued to live on in the hearts of the disciples. The New Testament eyewitness writers unanimously affirm that the very tomb in which Jesus had been buried was empty a few days later. The women had not gone to the wrong tomb and been mistaken in their assumption. Jesus had risen bodily from the dead.

Question 3. The second line of defense for Jesus' resurrection is his appearances to many people in different places and circumstances at different times.

Question 4. Jesus gives his disciples proof of his resurrection by showing them his hands and side. He pronounces his peace on them (a gift he had promised before his death). Jesus also gives them the Holy Spirit (v. 22). The Holy Spirit would come upon the disciples in power seven weeks later at the Feast of Pentecost (see Acts 2), but this empowerment would carry the disciples through the weeks ahead.

Question 5. Thomas could not be classified as an easily persuaded disciple who was caught up in some vague hope that Jesus had come back to life. Thomas had to be persuaded with undeniable proof.

Question 7. Jesus left Thomas with his doubts and questions for a whole week before he intervened. Sometimes it is best to leave the doubter in his or her struggle for a while. We think we have to provide all the answers to the skeptic immediately, instead of letting God work.

Question 8. Christians are persuaded today to believe in the resurrection by two factors: the clear testimony of Scripture and the inner witness of the Holy Spirit. Both are essential. It is not enough to believe the *fact* of the resurrection. We must receive the risen Christ into our lives and hearts.

Question 9. The message of the gospel is not only that Jesus died on the cross for our sins. The other essential element of the gospel is that Jesus rose from the dead. His resurrection proves that his claims are true and that his sacrifice was acceptable to the Father (read 1 Cor 15:1-8).

STUDY 13. JOHN 21. A WALK WITH A RESURRECTED MAN.

PURPOSE: To demonstrate Christ's ability to use us for his glory, no matter what our past failures have been.

Question 1. Some interpreters think that Peter and his friends were just taking some time off. Others see Peter's return to fishing as a return to his old way of life before he left everything to follow Jesus.

Question 3. In spite of his failure and his denial of Jesus, Peter still loved Jesus and wanted to be near him.

Question 5. It is not immediately apparent in most English translations, but in the Greek text of this passage, Jesus uses different words translated *love*. Jesus asks Peter twice, "Do you truly love me?" (vv. 15-16). In his question Jesus uses the verb *agapaō*. In his response, "Yes, Lord, you know that I love you," Peter uses the verb *phileō*. The third time Jesus asks the question, he too uses the verb *phileō*.

While some scholars hold that these two verbs are essentially synonymous in this passage, a case can be made that the change is intentional and significant. Those who hold the change to be significant stress the uniquely Christian use of *agapaō*, "to choose to love and to commit oneself sacrificially to the person loved."

Phileō, on the other hand, is generally used of love between friends and relatives; it stresses love based on relationship and emotional attachment.

If we accept that the difference is significant, then it appears that even though Peter's love was not all that Christ wanted it to be, Jesus was still willing to use Peter in ministry, saying, "Take care of my sheep."

Question 6. Genuine repentance is marked by humility and renewed love for Christ. Peter was no longer making the boastful statements he had made earlier. A new spirit of honesty is reflected in his words. Jesus, however, does not put Peter on probation. He gives him kingdom work to do.

Question 7. Perhaps Jesus began discussing death to keep Peter from being overly confident about his loyalty to Christ in the future. He also gave Peter assurance that even his death was under Christ's control.

We are never told in the Bible about Peter's death, but several early Christian writers give us the details. Peter was arrested at the order of the Roman emperor, Nero. When he was taken to be crucified, Peter asked to be crucified upside down. He did not consider himself worthy to die in the same manner as his Master. His request was granted.

Question 9. We will give an account of our lives to God, not to other people. That doesn't mean we ride roughshod over other people's lives, but ultimately we are responsible to please only one person, Jesus.

Douglas Connelly is a pastor, writer and speaker who lives in Davison, Michigan. He has written seventeen LifeGuide® Bible Studies as well as several books, including The Bible for Blockheads *and* Angels Around Us. *He and his wife, Karen, have three children and six grandchildren.*

Other LifeGuide® Bible Studies by Douglas Connelly

Angels: Standing Guard

Daniel: Spiritual Living in a Secular World

Elijah: Living Securely in an Unsecure World

Encountering Jesus

Following Jesus

Forgiveness: Making Peace with the Past

Good & Evil

Heaven: Finding Our True Home

Heroes of Faith

I Am: Discovering Who Jesus Is

The Lord's Prayer

Meeting the Spirit

The Messiah: The Texts Behind Handel's Masterpiece

Miracles: Signs of God's Glory

Names of God: Glimpses of His Character

The Twelve Disciples

LifeGuide® In Depth Bible Studies
by Douglas Connelly

A Deeper Look at Daniel: Spiritual Living in a Secular World

LifeGuide® in Depth Bible Studies

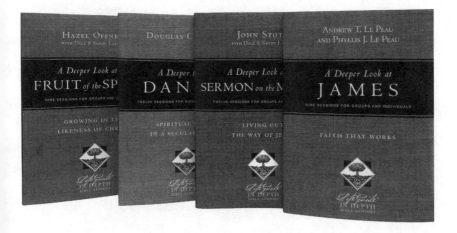

LifeGuide® in Depth Bible Studies help you to dive into the riches of Scripture by taking you further into themes and books than you might have gone before. As you see new connections between the Old and New Testament, gain an understanding of the historical and cultural background of passages, engage in creative exercises, and concretely apply what you've learned, you'll be amazed at the breadth of the knowledge and wisdom you gain and the transformation God can work in you as you meet him in his Word. Each session provides enough material for a week's worth of personal Scripture study along with a weekly group discussion guide that pulls all of the elements together.

These guides are based on and include the inductive Bible studies from the bestselling LifeGuide® Bible Study Series with over ten million copies sold. But they've been expanded for a new kind of study experience.

WHAT SHOULD
WE STUDY NEXT?

Since 1985 LifeGuide® Bible Studies have provided solid inductive Bible study content with field-tested questions that get groups talking—making for a one-of-a-kind Bible study experience. This series has more than 120 titles on Old and New Testament books, character studies, and topical studies. IVP's LifeGuide Finder is a great tool for searching for your next study topic: https://ivpress.com/lifeguidefinder.

Here are some ideas to get you started.

BIBLE BOOKS

An in-depth study of a Bible book is one of the richest experiences you could have in opening up the riches of Scripture. Many groups begin with a Gospel such as Mark or John. These guides are divided into two parts so that if twenty or twenty-six weeks feels like too much to do as once, the group can feel free to do half of the studies and take a break with another topic.

A shorter letter such as Philippians or Ephesians is also a great way to start. Shorter Old Testament studies include Ruth, Esther, and Job.

TOPICAL SERIES

Here are a few ideas of short series you might put together to cover a year of curriculum on a theme.

Christian Formation: *Christian Beliefs* (12 studies by Stephen D. Eyre), *Christian Character* (12 studies by Andrea Sterk & Peter Scazzero), *Christian Disciplines* (12 studies by Andrea Sterk & Peter Scazzero), *Evangelism* (12 studies by Rebecca Pippert & Ruth Siemens).

Building Community: *Christian Community* (10 studies by Rob Suggs), *Friendship* (10 studies by Carolyn Nystrom), *Spiritual Gifts* (12 studies by Charles & Anne Hummel), *Loving Justice* (12 studies by Bob and Carol Hunter).

GUIDES FOR SPECIFIC TYPES OF GROUPS

If you have a group that is serving a particular demographic, here are some specific ideas. Also note the list of studies for seekers on the back cover.

Women's Groups: *Women of the New Testament, Women of the Old Testament, Woman of God, Women & Identity, Motherhood*

Marriage and Parenting: *Marriage, Parenting, Grandparenting*